D1642947

GERTRUDE JEKYLL

Twigs Way

SHIRE PUBLICATIONS

Published in Great Britain in 2012 by Shire Publications Ltd, Midland House, West Way, Botley, Oxford OX2 0PH, United Kingdom.

44-02 23rd St, Suite 219, Long Island City, NY 11101

E-mail: shire@shirebooks.co.uk   www.shirebooks.co.uk

A CIP catalogue record for this book is available from the British Library.

Shire Library no. 663   •   ISBN-13: 978 0 74781 090 2

Twigs Way has asserted her right under the Copyright, Designs and Patents Act, 1988, to be identified as the author of this book.

Designed by Tony Truscott Designs, Sussex, UK and typeset in Perpetua and Gill Sans. Printed in China through Worldprint Ltd.

12 13 14 15 16   10 9 8 7 6 5 4 3 2 1

COVER IMAGE
The long border at Munstead Wood, by artist Helen Allingham.

TITLE PAGE IMAGE
Sir William Nicholson's famous portrait of Gertrude Jekyll had to be painted when she was not busy gardening. Between sittings he painted a portrait of her gardening boots!

CONTENTS PAGE IMAGE
A classic view of the Munstead Wood flower borders, c. 1906, included in the popular Edwardian *A Book of English Gardens*.

ACKNOWLEDGEMENTS
As ever, particular thanks are owed to Philip Norman at the Garden Museum for his assistance at every stage, and to Brent Elliott at the RHS Lindley Library. The Jekyll Estate has also been extremely helpful, and I would particularly like to thank Rosamund Wallinger at the Manor House, Upton Grey.

I would also like to thank the people who have allowed me to use illustrations, which are acknowledged as follows:

Greg Becker, pages 44, and 51 (bottom); Country Life Library, page 40; English Heritage, page 18; Francis Frith Collection, page 23; The Garden Museum: cover and pages 7, 8 (bottom), 15, 20–1, 22, 24, 36 (top), 36 (bottom), 38 (top), 42 (top), 43 (top), and 48; Godalming Museum, pages 8 (top), 16, and 21 (top); Caroline Holmes, pages 14, 17, and 50; The Jekyll Estate (and Surrey History centre), pages 4, and 6 (bottom); The Mallett Gallery / The Bridgeman Art Library, page 32; National Portrait Gallery, title page; The Wolseley Archive, Brighton and Hove Collections, page 22 (bottom); Christopher Wood Gallery / The Bridgeman Art Library, page 34.

Author's own collection: contents page and pages 6 (top), 9, 10, 11 (bottom), 13, 25, 26 (top), 26 (bottom), 27, 28, 29, 30, 31, 37 (top), 37 (bottom), 38 (bottom), 39, 42 (bottom), 43 (bottom), 45, 47, 49, 51 (top), and 54.

Shire Publications is supporting the Woodland Trust, the UK's leading woodland conservation charity, by funding the dedication of trees.

CONTENTS

EARLY LIFE, ART SCHOOL AND TRAVEL   4

ARTIST, GARDENER, CRAFTSWOMAN   10

FLOWERING AND MATURITY   18

BEYOND THE GARDEN GATE   32

AUTUMN OF A GARDENING LIFE   40

A GARDENING LEGACY   47

PLACES TO VISIT   53

FURTHER READING   55

INDEX   56

EARLY LIFE, ART SCHOOL AND TRAVEL

It must have been at about seven years of age that I first learnt to know and love a primrose copse.

'Epilogue' from *A Gardener's Testament*, Country Life, 1937.

BORN IN Grafton Street, London, on a late November day in 1843, Gertrude Jekyll was the fifth of seven children in the family of Edward Joseph Jekyll, retired captain in the Grenadier Guards, and his wife Julia, daughter of the banker Charles Hammersley. In later life Jekyll recalled her early London childhood as one of daisy chains and newly cut grass in the gardens of Berkeley Square, and long walks among bright golden dandelions in Green Park. The family move to West Surrey in 1848 seemed to continue this flowery theme, adding to the delights of London gardens a countryside of woods and heaths, ponds and meadows, and, of course, wild flowers. With her brothers away at school, and her only sister seven years her senior, Jekyll was allowed a carefree existence exploring the countryside and the characters within it, subjects which would fascinate her throughout her life. Her own character as it developed was slightly 'different' – her father called her 'a queer child' – and she had an independence born of solitariness.

It was at the family home at Bramley House, near Guildford, that a governess gave her a copy of the book that was to prove fundamental to her life: *Flowers of the Field*, by the Reverend C. A. Johns, President of the Winchester Literary and Scientific Society. *Flowers of the Field*, of which Jekyll was eventually to own and wear out three copies, was a book of wild-flower identification based on the botanical system. As Jekyll later explained in her book *Children and Gardens* (1908), she did not realise this as a child and used instead to compare plants she had collected with each illustration one by one, having no idea of the system of genera and families. Bramley House itself had extensive gardens, including parterres and bedding in traditional Victorian style, a shrubbery, rhododendrons, a 'verbena garden', and a fernery and rustic bridge. A walled kitchen garden, an acre in extent,

Opposite:
Gertrude Jekyll
aged nineteen.
(Courtesy of the
Jekyll Estate.)

VIOLA CANINA, *and* V. ODORATA.

Viola canina, the wild dog's-tooth violet, as illustrated in the Reverend C. A. Johns's book *Flowers of the Field.*

provided fruits and vegetables for the family and, as her brother Herbert recalled, included 'a long range of greenhouses and an abundance of peaches, nectarines, plums, cherries and pears'. Beyond the gardens were ponds, including the old mill pond of 4 acres, and an orchard and dairy with a small herd of Alderney cows. Jekyll seems always to have retained a fondness for the village of Bramley. Years later she returned with her then colleague Edwin Lutyens, who designed Millmead House for her in Snowdenham Lane (Bramley); it was a speculative development between the two, with Jekyll designing the gardens.

The idyllic country life in Surrey was supplemented by holidays on the Isle of Wight, and eventually (at the age of twelve) in Bavaria. In Bavaria her father recorded that she spoke German well and was an excellent traveller, no doubt well prepared by the governesses who schooled her in languages, art and music. Art in particular attracted her, a skill perhaps inherited from her grandfather Joseph Jekyll (1753–1837), a Fellow of the Royal Society of Arts. As she grew older she spent much time painting and studying in a small hut constructed in the garden of Bramley House, presaging perhaps the later 'Hut' that Lutyens constructed for her at Munstead Wood. In 1861 she enrolled as a pupil at the South Kensington Schools of Art, journeying up from Surrey for classes which included applied

Iron Lane, Bramley, Surrey, *c.* 1860s, by Gertrude Jekyll. (Courtesy of the Jekyll Estate.)

and decorative arts as well as life studies from classical statues (partially draped for modesty). Her sister-in-law Agnes Jekyll was later to describe her as 'a pioneer spirit' leading the way in women's right to independence and self-expression, and this is apparent in her bold adoption of the art world as her own.

Gertrude's mother, although interested in art, leaned more towards music and had been an accomplished pupil of Mendelssohn, while her father collected Etruscan vases and life-size classical statues of cats. Family friends were also drawn from the worlds of art and culture, through both her parents and her brothers. Herbert was a friend of Robert Louis Stevenson, who commemorated the friendship by using the surname in his famous novel *The Strange Case of Dr Jekyll and Mr Hyde*. Charles Newton, Keeper of Greek and Roman Antiquities at the British Museum, was a friend of her father, as was his wife Mary Newton, herself an artist and friend of Ruskin. It was with the Newtons that Gertrude travelled, in 1863, to Corfu, Rhodes, Athens, Smyrna, Constantinople (Istanbul), and other Greek islands before returning home via Marseilles and Paris. Again she appears to have been an admirably calm traveller, taking in her stride dangerous roads, brigands, earthquakes and the wreck of their ship the day after they disembarked.

Jehu Driving Furiously, by Gertrude Jekyll. When she was young Jekyll would act as 'charioteer', driving a small pony cart with her brothers inside. A family friend at that period was Henry Austen Layard, the archaeologist who excavated at Nineveh.

Arriving home on Boxing Day 1863 at the age of twenty, Gertrude was now more than ever committed to the world of the artist. Her upper-middle-class background, and the very fact of her being a woman, meant that she was not expected to follow a particular career or make a living, and with the security of the family home always available for her, she could devote herself to study of the arts and crafts. The next ten years of her life were full of excitement as she moved within the circles of the then burgeoning Arts and Crafts Movement, taking on board their political and moral ideas as well as their artistic influence. Ruskin, William Morris, G. F. Watts and the influential Blumenthals (whose home Jekyll shared on her visits to London) were all well known to her, and through them the Pre-Raphaelites and the circles around the painters Hercules Brabazon Brabazon, George Leslie and Barbara Leigh Smith (later Madame Bodichon). It was Madame Bodichon who invited Gertrude to advise on the interior decoration of Girton College, Cambridge, when it was founded in 1873. Embroidery, marquetry and carving were

Gertrude Jekyll's craft skills enabled her to make both decorative and utilitarian objects. This handmade key ring, now in the Garden Museum, bears a monogram of her own design.

among her many accomplishments at this time, and she was commissioned to embroider the silk panels for the Duke of Westminster's new wing at Eaton Hall, as well as cushions for the London home of Lord Leighton. She also designed and executed much of the interior of the Blumenthals' house at 43 Hyde Park Gate, a fashionable gathering point for artists and musicians, including HRH Princess Louise, daughter of Queen Victoria. The design for the Blumenthals comprised orange trees and peacocks, with a ceiling decoration of orange leaves. Later she was to add photography to this list of arts and crafts accomplishments.

Jekyll's life was very much London-based during this period, but with time also spent abroad, in particular in Switzerland with the Blumenthals, or Algiers with Madame Bodichon, and it may be no coincidence that these were the years when her family moved away from her beloved Surrey to Wargrave in Berkshire. The move was not a successful one, lasting only eight years (1868–76), but was perhaps important in 'liberating' Gertrude Jekyll from the comforts of the home scene.

In his book *Our River,* the artist George Leslie recorded his impressions of Jekyll at this intensely creative period of her life:

> a young lady of such singular and remarkable accomplishments ... Clever and witty in conversation, active and energetic in mind and body, and possessed of artistic talents of no common order ... there is hardly any useful handicraft the mysteries of which she has not mastered, carving, modelling, house-painting, carpentry, smith's work, repoussé work, gilding, wood inlaying, embroidery, gardening and all manner of herb and culture ... her artistic taste is very great.

George Leslie's reference to Jekyll's particular interest in gardening and herbs is repeated again in an entry in the Blumethals' chalet party guest books from Sonzier in Switzerland, where a rhyme records that:

> Miss Jekyll
> Went up a hill
> To fetch a flower she sought there.
> The price in town is half a crown
> For each like root she bought there.

Elsewhere a single line written by her brother in the chalet book records that she would 'Mount hill and fetch the maidenhair'. Jekyll had recorded sending back *Iris albicans* from her travels with the Newtons in Greece in 1863–4, and again collected plants on her Italian travels in 1872 and 1876. This fascination with plant collecting had remained constant through the years of art and crafts, combining with architecture and painting. In his memoir of Jekyll published in 1944, Sir Herbert Baker wrote that she saw 'the art and creation of home-making as a whole in relation to Life, the best simple English country life … in the building and its furnishing and their homely craftsmanship, in the garden uniting the house with surrounding nature; all in harmony … ' and this was the period of her life in which this harmonic combination of arts, crafts and plants first came to fruition. Jekyll spent much of the following years balancing her love of arts and crafts with her burgeoning knowledge and skill in gardening, keeping a foot in each border. Her eyesight began to fail in 1891, finally forcing her to abandon her original love of painting and devote herself entirely to her plants and gardens and the crafts associated with them.

Jekyll's arts training allowed her to appreciate contrasting and complementary colours as well as contrasting foliage types, as seen here at Hestercombe, Somerset.

ARTIST, GARDENER, CRAFTSWOMAN

What is needed for doing the best gardening is something of an artist's training.'

Gertrude Jekyll, preface to *The Well Considered Garden* by Mrs Francis King.

THE YEARS BETWEEN 1875 and 1891 were ones of shift and change in Jekyll's life. In 1876 her beloved father died, and, with his death and the marriages of her elder brothers and sister Carrie, there were now only Gertrude, her mother and her brother Herbert at the family home at Wargrave. It was decided that the family would move back to Surrey, and Munstead Heath, near Godalming, was selected as the location for a new house that was to be built for them. The site was chosen because of its proximity both to their original family home of Bramley House and to Godalming station. Building works at Munstead included not only the house but also a kitchen garden; in the autumn of 1877 fruit trees were transplanted from Wargrave to Munstead, which must have been a shock for them, coming from the chalk of Berkshire to the acidic sands of Surrey. It was, however, this very detail of landscape which Jekyll adored. In a letter to the artist George Leslie she wrote, 'I only hated Berkshire because it was not Surrey, and chalk because it was not sand.'

In 1875 Gertrude Jekyll made her first contributions to the respected periodical *The Garden*, edited by William Robinson, marking the real start of her commitment to the art and craft of gardening (although she had been advising friends and family for several years before this). Robinson, a tireless campaigner for the delights of the hardy English flower garden, and equally tireless campaigner against the artificialities of the outmoded 'bedding system' of annual plantings, owned and edited *The Garden* and frequently included contributions by artists and writers such as William Morris and John Ruskin. (On the death of Ruskin in January 1900, *The Garden* carried an appreciation of him written by Robinson.) Gertrude Jekyll would have been known to Robinson both through their joint connections with the Arts

Opposite:
A classic view of Munstead Wood, c. 1906, combining the Lutyens seat with the garden court. Clematis trails over the overhang of the jettied upper floor, and a pot of lilies sits by the steps.

Miss Jekyll was an avid plant hunter even on her early travels. (Cartoon by Lionel Benson.)

Gravetye Manor, Sussex, home of William Robinson, editor of *The Garden* and friend of Gertrude Jekyll.

and Crafts world and also her plant collecting, which, although only in its infancy at this stage in her life, was directed at exactly the topic that interested Robinson, the introduction into English gardens of wild plants and hardy plants from Britain and Europe. In 1883 Jekyll travelled to Capri, painting and plant collecting, using a specially designed pick to collect plants such as *Lithospermum rosmarinifolium, Crocus imperati, Campanula fragilis* and *Rosa sempervirens* from the rocky slopes of the island; following this, she travelled to the Pyrenees, where she collected *Primula villosa* and *Fritillaria pyrenaica*. Her plant-collecting antics were captured in cartoons by the pianist Lionel Benson, who was also part of the cultural circle centred on the Blumenthals.

In the autumn of 1877 the new house at Munstead was completed and Jekyll and her mother were able finally to move in, ending what she was later to recall as eight years of 'perpetual homesickness' for the Surrey heaths and woodlands. Many of the plants had been transferred from Wargrave, but Jekyll took advantage of this opportunity to create gardens in the style discussed in the pages of *The Garden*. The gardens included a hardy flower garden, an alpine garden, a bank of Scotch briars, a grove of azaleas,

rhododendron plantings, an orchard, and a kitchen garden (fronted by a hardy flower border), as well as areas of heathland and grass walks. A reserve garden was used as a nursery. Later she was to describe this creation of a new garden as 'doing living pictures with land and trees and flowers'. By 1880 the garden was developed enough to draw the admiration of visitors, including Edward Woodall, Dean Samuel Reynolds Hole, and of course William Robinson (who first came in 1880 with Dean Hole). A close neighbour and early visitor, Harry Mangles, was a rhododendron specialist, utilising the sandy soils of the heaths. The garden at Munstead retained large areas of woodland, as later would her own Munstead Wood, and paths had been created through this to lead from the house to the wilder areas. By 1881 Jekyll's horticultural renown had grown sufficiently for her to be asked to act as a judge at the Royal Horticultural Society (RHS) Show, precursor to the famous Chelsea Flower Show.

That same year her artistic circle also expanded with the marriage of her brother Herbert to Agnes Graham of Glasgow, daughter of the art collector and MP William Graham. Through his father-in-law's connections Herbert was now drawn further into the world of Brabazon and Ruskin, Rossetti and Burne-Jones, connections that drew Gertrude Jekyll with them. The standing of Jekyll's own craft work at this period was such that two pieces, a tortoiseshell casket and an iron tray, were bought by the Museum of Science and Art (in 1899 renamed the Victoria and Albert Museum) as examples of the best of the age. In addition to these traditional crafts Jekyll also took up the relatively new art of photography, producing her first images in 1885. This new interest was approached in her usual thorough way, with series of images, of different exposures and developing procedures, being overlaid in annotated books for future reference. Photography, and in particular photographs of the

Miss Jekyll frequently used images taken around Munstead Wood to illustrate her articles and books. In these she never specified the location. This image is taken from an article on lilies printed in *The Garden* in 1901.

traditional Surrey landscape and architecture, was to be a lifelong interest and in later years many of these images were used to illustrate her own books. Seeking to repel unwanted visitors to Munstead Wood in later life, she would suggest instead that they refer to the illustrations in her books, which 'were secured at different times of year … so that anything the garden can show or teach can be better seen in books than on the ground itself'.

In about 1882–3 the threat of building work on land adjoining Munstead House appears to have influenced Jekyll's mother (now in her seventies) to purchase the area herself, with an eventual view of providing her daughter with her own establishment. Mrs Jekyll may also have been influenced in her decision by the increasing tide of horticultural and artistic visitors to Munstead House, and the youthful habits of her daughter, who, she had once remarked, clumped through the best rooms of their Surrey house in her gardening boots! The area known as Munstead Wood comprised 15 acres to the north of Munstead itself and was, as Munstead itself had originally been, mainly sandy heath and birch woodland. For the first few years there appear to have been no plans for actually building a separate house on the site, and

The restored lupin (and foxglove!) borders at Munstead Wood.

what plans there were for a garden lacked the focus of a building. Jekyll later confessed that there had been no definite plan for the garden and that this had resulted in many awkward angles when the house was finally created.

Whatever the original reason for the delay in the building of the house, it can only be described as serendipitous, for it allowed for the eventual creation of house and garden by what was to become one of the greatest ever partnerships: that between Gertrude Jekyll and Edwin Lutyens. Jekyll first met Edwin Lutyens at a tea party, hosted by her neighbour Harry Mangles at his home, Littleworth Cross, in 1889. It was a party of gardening friends and the young Lutyens may well have felt slightly lost, later recalling 'the silver kettle and the conversation reflecting the rhododendrons'. Little was exchanged between the two future partners. It was only as Jekyll was leaving that there was any intimation that this was to be a particular friendship – on the steps of her pony cart, with reins in hand, Jekyll turned and issued an invitation to Lutyens for tea at Munstead the following Saturday. At first sight the friendship that blossomed between Lutyens and Jekyll seems unlikely. She was an accomplished artist, now almost forty-six, a slightly eccentric, and perhaps solitary, figure among the lively Arts and Crafts circle in which she moved. She was already suffering from the severe myopia that was soon to change her life and must have been feeling its effects, with headaches and eye strain. Edwin Lutyens (known as Ned) was, on the other hand, at the start of his career. Twenty-six years her junior, he came from a large family of thirteen children and, although he had suffered from delicate health when young, was by now marked only by shyness – something Miss Jekyll never appeared to have suffered from.

Lutyens had fixed on a career in architecture early on in his life, studying it from the age of sixteen at the National Art Training School in South Kensington (also known as the South Kensington Schools of Art, later to become the Royal College of Art). After two years at the school he moved to the offices of architects Ernest George and Harold Peto, staying only a year before setting up on his own in 1888–9. When he met Miss Jekyll he had just completed carrying out

In this letter, dated 1928, Gertrude Jekyll recalls how 'when I was young I had hoped to be a painter' but adds that bad eyesight forced her to give up that dream.

15

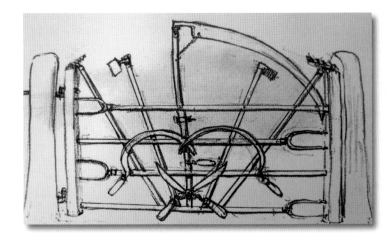

The 'silly gate'
of garden tools
reflects Jekyll's
love of fun and
eye for design.
(Courtesy of the
Jekyll Estate.)

alterations at The Corner, Thursley, Surrey, and was about to commence on the design of Crooksbury, in Farnham, Surrey, for Arthur Chapman. Jekyll made some 'tentative suggestions' for the garden at Crooksbury, but it was with Lutyens's next commission, Chinthurst Hill for Miss Guthrie, that the partnership really commenced, with Jekyll laying out the terraces. Watching the planning and development of these new houses must have inspired Jekyll, as by 1894 she had at last begun to plan the building of her own house at Munstead Wood. Her mother's Munstead House had been designed by John James Stevenson, an adherent of the Society for the Protection of Ancient Buildings (SPAB), founded by Philip Webb in 1877. Webb had designed Red House, Bexleyheath, for William Morris in 1859, and, closer to Jekyll, Conyhurst, Surrey, in 1885 and Standen, West Sussex, in 1892–4, all in the Arts and Crafts style. Munstead Wood was also to be in this style, but, instead of Webb, Lutyens was to be the architect.

The first stage of the project was the construction of what became known as 'The Hut'; this was to be used as a workshop-cum-studio and eventual living space for the years while the main house was being created. The Hut was completed in November 1894 and Jekyll began to use it as her main residence in the following year, after the death of her mother, when her brother and his family inherited the original Munstead House. The following year saw Lutyens's most prestigious commission yet, and one that was to establish his career: an additional wing to the Ferry Inn at Rosneath for HRH Princess Louise (wife of the then Marquess of Lorne). However, the Munstead project was not neglected and Lutyens made frequent visits to discuss and debate, sometimes heatedly, the plans for the house. By 1896 he was not visiting alone, but was bringing his future wife, Lady Emily Lytton, to meet his beloved 'Bumps', as he had nicknamed Miss Jekyll. It is from

Lady Emily's accounts of their journeys together that we get an impression of Jekyll at this period, now in her fifties and increasingly focused on her home and garden: kind and enchanting, fascinating and fun, but also a little scary, and already the plump shape that characterised her later years, making 'Bumps' an appropriate nickname. An early nickname used at the Blumenthal chalet parties had been 'Steigal', followed by 'Oozle' (or 'Woozle') by Lutyens, and later 'Tante Suite', a play on their relationship being similar to that of a kindly aunt and her nephew!

Munstead Wood house was finally completed in 1897 and Jekyll moved from The Hut to the house, where she was to settle for the rest of her life. The garden around the house had already been laid out with a spring garden, terraces, green wood walk, flower borders, and an area of azaleas and rhododendrons, as well as discrete borders and gardens set aside for specific species or particular seasons, such as the September Michaelmas daisy borders, the iris and lupin borders, or the June garden by The Hut. Jekyll's all-important gardens had been created with, in her own words, a 'hole in the centre of the ground' left for the house. With the completion of that house this now became a whole.

The lawn and garden front of Munstead Wood.

FLOWERING AND MATURITY

This garden belongs to an artist in the highest sense of the word, and is one in which hours, days, and months could be spent among its beauties. Every moment leads to the discovery of a new colour effect or audacious colour contrast ... the amazingly beautiful result obtainable by skilled eyes and clever hands.

M. Gloag, *A Book of English Gardens* (1906), describing Munstead Wood.

WITH THE COMPLETION of her new house and gardens one aspect of Gertrude Jekyll's life now became settled, but her garden design and writing were rapidly taking on new challenges and new directions. She was already carrying out small planting plans and designs for an extended network of friends and family. In 1888, for example, she sent 'rough sketch plans' for the 'spaces at disposal suggested' in the garden of Lady Wolseley, then at Hampton Lodge, Farnham, Surrey. Her writing was also in demand. In addition to her articles for *The Garden* (for which periodical she became editor in 1900, taking over from William Robinson), the *Edinburgh Review* and *The Guardian* now welcomed her contributions. It was the collected articles from *The Guardian* that were to form the basis for her first book, *Wood and Garden,* subtitled 'Notes and thoughts, practical and critical, of a working amateur, with seventy-one photographs by the author'. By this time her collection of photographs encompassed not only the development of Munstead but gardens and plants in all locations. The success of that first book prompted the series of other titles that followed under the auspices of *Country Life* and the publishers Longmans. *Home and Garden* (1900) was succeeded by *Lilies for English Gardens, Wall and Water Gardens* (both 1901), with *Roses for English Gardens* the following year. A slight change of direction in 1904 allows an insight into her fascination with the English countryside and country traditions in the publication of *Old West Surrey*, as well as her collaboration with the artist George Samuel Elgood, *Some English Gardens*. The years 1907–16 saw books on *Flower Decoration in the House, Children and*

Opposite:
Gertrude Jekyll, captured unusually in a patterned dress, in the Deanery Gardens, Sonning, c. 1901.

Gardens, Colour in the Flower Garden (perhaps her most popular book), and *Annuals and Biennials*. The magnificent *Gardens for Small Country Houses* (1912) was published with Lawrence Weaver at a period when both were writing for *Country Life* (Weaver was the architectural editor), and the book is filled with images from the pages of that prestigious periodical.

Back in the late 1890s, when *Wood and Garden* was being written, Jekyll was not yet a household name, although well known in horticultural circles. The writer Marie Theresa Earle, herself working on the first of her many books in 1897, said in *Pot Pourri from a Surrey Garden*, 'I trust that before long these articles [by Jekyll, in *The Guardian*] will be republished in book form, for every word in them deserves attention and consideration'. Mrs Earle, writing under her husband's initials 'C. W.', also noted perceptively that:

This plan, dating from the 1920s, is typical of the hundreds Jekyll produced. The measurements are marked off, and drifts of plants indicated and named, with numbers of plants and notes on their procurement.

[Miss Jekyll] has gone through the stage so common to all ambitious and enthusiastic amateurs, of trying to grow everything, and of often wasting much precious room in growing inferior plants, or plants which, even though they may be worth growing in themselves, are yet not worth the care and feeding which a light soil necessitates if they are to be successful.

The comment on 'light soil' was especially relevant as by then Jekyll was running a small nursery from Munstead Wood, selling surplus plants suitable for light soils. Two years later, Jekyll's *Wood and Garden* referred in turn to 'the many valuable suggestions in Mrs Earle's delightful book'.

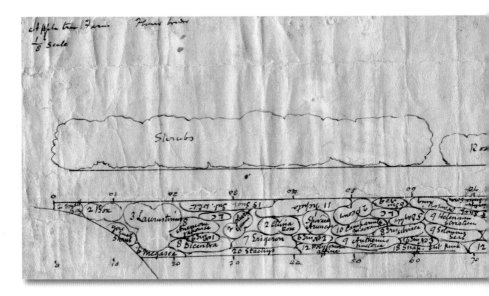

Theresa Earle and Gertrude Jekyll were also linked outside the world of gardening, as both had attended the South Kensington Schools of Art and both were within the Ruskin circle. Emily Lytton (married to Edwin Lutyens in 1897 and almost equally at home with 'Bumps') was also a

Banner for the Godalming branch of the Women's Suffrage movement, designed and embroidered by Gertrude Jekyll.

niece of Theresa Earle. It was Emily who declared that '"Bumps" was a very good name; she is very fat and stumpy, dresses rather like a man, little tiny eyes, very nearly blind, and big spectacles.' The Lutyens children referred to Jekyll as 'Aunt Bumps'. Theresa Earle's other niece was Constance Lytton, the suffragette, and, although not a member herself, Jekyll created a banner for the Godalming Branch of the Association of Women's Suffrage Societies.

During this period, and for much of her life, Jekyll's closest female colleague and friend was the horticulturalist Ellen Willmott. Miss Willmott (1858–1934) worked within the new English garden style, utilising hardy, herbaceous and alpine plantings rather than tender bedding. William Robinson was an admirer of her garden at Warley Place, Essex, recording that 'I have never seen anything more beautiful in nature or in gardens than the grassy banks planted with the smaller and rarer Narcissi in the gardens at Warley Place'. From her gardens at Warley Place (Essex), Aix-les-Bains

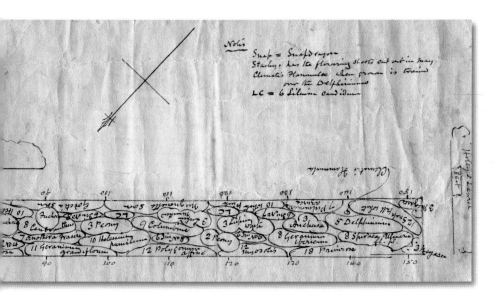

THE "COUNTRY LIFE"
LIBRARY.

ROSES FOR ENGLISH GARDENS.

BY

GERTRUDE JEKYLL

AND

EDWARD MAWLEY.

PUBLISHED BY

"COUNTRY LIFE"   GEORGE NEWNES, LTD
20, TAVISTOCK STREET,   7-12, SOUTHAMPTON STREET,
COVENT GARDEN, W.C.   COVENT GARDEN, W.C.
1902.

(France), and Ventimiglia (Italy), Ellen Willmott kept up a constant stream of new varieties of plants, winning RHS medals and funding plant hunters in China and the Middle East until her vast fortune ran out. Gertrude Jekyll's rather constrained finances did not allow such luxuries, although her brother Herbert, living with his family at Munstead House, subscribed to the plant expeditions of Frank Kingdon-Ward and received plants in return. In her book *Children and Gardens* (1908) Jekyll described Ellen Willmott as 'the greatest of living women-gardeners', while, in his address on the occasion of their both receiving the Victoria Medal of Honour in 1897, Dean Reynolds Hole called Miss Willmott 'Queen of Hearts' and Miss Jekyll 'Queen of Spades'. A photograph by Miss Willmott of their mutual friend, the writer Elizabeth von Arnim (author of *Elizabeth's German Garden*), sitting in a garden playhouse, accompanied this compliment. Ellen Willmott also provided much photographic material and text for Jekyll's *Roses for English*

Roses for English Gardens reflected the Edwardian love of roses and rose gardens, as well as Jekyll's own love of 'Monthly' (China) roses.

The list of patrons of the Glynde School for Lady Gardeners included many of Gertrude Jekyll's close gardening friends.

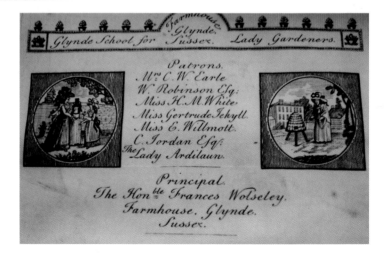

Gardens in 1902 (with Edward Mawley providing the practical information on pruning, planting and propagation).

In 1897 Willmott and Jekyll were together the first women to be awarded the prestigious Royal Horticultural Society Victoria Medal of Honour. They were also both patrons of the Glynde School for Lady Gardeners, founded by Viscountess Frances Wolseley in *c.* 1901, as were Theresa Earle, William Robinson, Lady Ardilaun (another passionate gardener), and Miss Henrietta White, Lady Principal of Alexandra College, Dublin. Jekyll had held back slightly when first approached to be a patron, on account of the many calls on her time, but readily assented on the understanding that she would be one of several patrons. In 1908 Jekyll collaborated with students from the Glynde School at the Edward VII Sanatorium in Midhurst, Sussex, Jekyll designing much of the gardens, and the students carrying out the planting and building some of the stone walls which formed part of her schemes. Many of the plants used were brought from her nurseries at Munstead Wood, including aromatic herbs thought to benefit the patients, who also worked in the gardens.

The years between 1899 and 1914 were perhaps Jekyll's most fruitful, producing eleven of her thirteen books, numerous articles, and the most prolific period of her collaboration with Edwin Lutyens – a collaboration which was sadly impacted on by the First World War. In *Wall and Water Gardens* (1901) Jekyll wrote:

The Edward VII Sanatorium gardens at Midhurst, Sussex, were designed by Miss Jekyll and planted by the students of the Glynde School for Lady Gardeners.

Opposite:
The wild garden
at Upton Grey,
Hampshire; a rare
survival of one of
Jekyll's informal
water gardens.

The whole question of the relation of vegetation to architecture is a very large one, and to know what to place where, and when to stop, and when to abstain altogether, requires much knowledge on both sides … The truth appears to be that for the best building and planting … the architect and the gardeners must have some knowledge of each other's business, and each must regard with feelings of kindly reverence the unknown domains of the other's higher knowledge.

The house at Munstead, she noted, had been achieved 'in the happiest way possible, a perfect understanding between the architect, the builder, and the proprietor'. These sentiments provided an ideal foundation for the partnership between Jekyll and Lutyens, which was born against a background of much acrimony between architects and gardeners, most notably in the exchanges between William Robinson and Reginald Blomfield, author of *The Formal Garden in England* (1892). It was on to these troubled waters that Jekyll had attempted to pour oil when she wrote in the *Edinburgh Review* (July 1896) that:

Gertrude Jekyll
published *Wall and
Water Gardens* in
1901, and
frequently used
drystone walling
for planting, even
learning to build
her own walls.
Here she indicates
their use to a
client.

The formal army are architects to a man; they are undoubtedly right in upholding the simple dignity and sweetness and quiet beauty of the old formal garden but … they ignore the immense resources that are the precious possession of modern gardeners, and therefore offer no sort of encouragement to their utilisation … We cannot now, with all this treasure at our feet, neglect it and refuse it the gratefully appreciative use it deserves. We cannot go back a century or two and stop short at the art of the formal gardener …

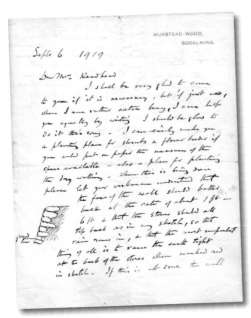

Jekyll forged a middle way between the two warring parties, and then led by example. Harold Falkner (originally apprenticed at the offices of Reginald Blomfield himself) adored Munstead Wood and described it as 'partly formal, partly controlled wild'.

After the completion of the house at Munstead Wood Jekyll and Lutyens's next collaboration was to become one of their most famous: the Deanery Gardens, Sonning, Berkshire, owned by Edward Hudson (founder of *Country Life*) as a weekend retreat. Lutyens created a symphony of light and shade, with pergolas, courtyards, rills

Having learnt
how to construct
drystone walling,
Gertrude Jekyll
combined this
craft with her
gardening skills
in the planting of
walls.

The restored
gardens at Le Bois
des Moutiers,
Normandy.

and walks. Within this Jekyll added soft colours and grey foliage in borders and over the dry stone walls, with rambling roses everywhere softening the new brickwork. The features found at the Deanery – rills, pergolas, courts, curved stairs – all became hallmarks of the Lutyens/Jekyll partnership. In 1898 Lutyens was asked to create an Arts and Crafts-style house from a rather plain brick house at Le Bois des Moutiers, Normandy, France (the connection may have come through Theresa Earle, who knew the owner, Guillaume Mallet) and in 1904 Gertrude Jekyll was asked to provide planting schemes for the gardens, which still survive today.

Smaller house and garden commissions followed at Marsh Court, Hampshire (1901–4) and Millmead, Surrey (1904–7), before the stunningly sited Hestercombe in Somerset provided a unique opportunity to display the skills of their partnership. Set in the Quantock Hills, overlooking the Vale of Taunton, Hestercombe was a Victorian mansion set within gardens dating from both the eighteenth century and the Victorian era. The owner, the Hon. E. W. Portman, desired a formal garden to the

Hestercombe Gardens, now restored to their former glory, display the combined skills of Lutyens and Jekyll – seen here in late summer splendour.

27

front of the property and Lutyens created the framework of a series of terraces, encompassing a 125-foot-square sunken plot, with flanking water terraces and a pergola allowing views across the vale. This framework was constructed of local stone, in mellow greys and yellows, and Jekyll complemented this with a planting scheme that both echoed it and contrasted with it, with silver-grey foliage plants, her signature *Bergenia cordifolia*, and striking seasonal planting including cannas and gladioli. In 1906 the garden was further extended with a small raised 'Dutch' garden and a William and Mary-style orangery by Lutyens.

Folly Farm, Sulhamstead, Berkshire, created in 1906 and then again for a new owner in 1912, was less grand than Hestercombe but perhaps the most imaginative of their collaborative projects. Lutyens created courts and parterres, long vistas and sunken gardens. The 1912 reworking included the now famous canal, based on the Dutch-inspired gardens of the seventeenth century, such as Westbury Court, Gloucestershire. Jekyll planted into this framework with her famous rule of always choosing the plant for the place and the conditions.

The rills and pools at Hestercombe are typical Lutyens and Jekyll features, combining architecture and planting.

Dianthus and lavender spilled over warm stone, while away from the formal areas rhododendrons created a wilder walk similar to that at Munstead.

The commission that perhaps most challenged Jekyll's plantsmanship was that of Lindisfarne Castle, Northumberland. Purchased by Edward Hudson as a weekend retreat from his duties on *Country Life*, it was appropriate that he should seek advice from Lutyens and Jekyll on the restoration of the castle and the creation of a garden. Originally a grand water garden was envisaged, with the existing small walled garden turned instead into a tennis court, but financial sense prevailed and it was for the old walled area (75 feet 'square') that Jekyll eventually created a design, even visiting the site despite the long distance and her deteriorating eyesight. Roses, hollyhocks, sunflowers and gladioli were located in borders below the sheltering walls, while more exposed beds contained lower growing perennials, including her hallmark, *Stachys byzantina*. The site was a difficult one, with wild salty winds, and the planting had to be adapted when some plants failed. Jekyll was to encounter similar problems at the Irish site of Lambay Castle, Co. Dublin, another island site, although here the native wild flowers almost outshone the garden planting: the architectural writer Lawrence Weaver recorded that 'Lambay is an island of flowers'.

Despite the undoubted success of their collaboration, even at the height of their partnership Jekyll still undertook commissions directly for clients or with other architects. In 1907 she was consulted by a Mr Best on the gardens at the Manor House, Upton Grey, Hampshire. Best was actually the tenant of the property, which was owned by Charles Holme, a famous art

Stachys byzantina was one of Miss Jekyll's favourite plants, providing textured grey foliage throughout the seasons.

Part of the
restored wall
garden at the
Manor House,
Upton Grey,
Hampshire.

collector, who had been responsible for the renovation of the house and site. The gardens occupied almost 5 acres, with a formal garden at the rear and a wild garden to the front. Drystone terraces, pergolas, and a formal rose lawn, as well as the long borders, allowed Jekyll to include almost all her favourite planting combinations, as well as the naturalistic planting in the pond and grass of the wild area. The 1980s restoration of the gardens has rightly made this one of the most famous of Jekyll's commissions, as it combines the terracing of Hestercombe with the colour expertise of Munstead Wood and the charm of her other wild garden and pond planting at Vann, Surrey. Jekyll's own woodland gardens at Munstead were able to provide much of the planting for these wild gardens (and the basis for her expertise). At Vann, designed in 1912, Jekyll offered to supply 1,500 plants, including ferns, hostas, bog myrtle, fritillarias and marsh marigolds – quite an accomplishment for a nursery based among the sandy Surrey heathlands!

During this most active period of her garden career, before the First World War, Jekyll was designing four or five gardens a year, many for friends or friends of friends in the Arts and Crafts circle, others for clients of architects, and some for clients with no obvious connection who appear to have contacted her through her writings in *Country Life*. Thanks to Jekyll's position as garden writer for *Country Life*, and Lutyens's creation of the Deanery Gardens, Plumpton Place and Lindisfarne Castle for E. H. Hudson, their work was featured frequently in the pages of what was fast becoming the most respected and fashionable periodical. Between 1907 and his death in 1933, the architectural editor at *Country Life* was H. Avray Tipping, an admirer not only of Lutyens but of his fellow writer (and fellow gardener) Gertrude Jekyll. Tipping wrote of Jekyll that she '… marshalled her wide knowledge and tasteful mastery of the best horticulture into an ordered array of facts and suggestions that have been of infinite assistance to thousands of amateur garden makers and maintainers'. By profiling Lutyens's houses, Tipping also promoted the work of Jekyll among those who could afford not only the facts and suggestions in her books, but to commission the actual artist gardener herself.

The restored Gertrude Jekyll borders at the Manor House, Upton Grey, Hampshire.

BEYOND THE GARDEN GATE

The general muddle and want of distinct intention that is so frequent in gardens ... is ... so wasteful because a place may be full of fine plants, grandly grown, but if they are mixed up without a definite scheme they only produce an unsatisfactory effect, instead of composing together into a harmonious picture.

Gertrude Jekyll, in *Gardens for Small Country Houses* (1912).

A s Munstead Wood literally blossomed, it began to attract not only visitors from the gardening community, but also artists anxious to capture the mix of formality and cottage-garden style that made up the newly fashionable 'old-world' garden. By working with the structures of artistic theory, using the colour wheel to create contrasts, hues and complementary colours, Jekyll had in turn created a garden that made an ideal picture. Artists now flocked to the gardens (and other gardens designed by her) to record these masterpieces of colour and texture. Included among the visitors to Munstead Wood were Helen Allingham, Thomas Hunn and George Samuel Elgood, each of whom specialised in watercolours of gardens or rural life. Roger Fry, a member of the Bloomsbury Group, also visited several times in 1910–11.

Helen Allingham (1848–1926) is now best known for her paintings of thatched cottages and idyllic cottage gardens. Originally from Burton upon Trent, Allingham had attended the Royal Academy Schools, London, in 1867, and had moved to Witley in Surrey following her marriage to the Irish poet William Allingham. In 1874 two of Allingham's rural watercolours were accepted for the Royal Academy Summer Exhibition (where Jekyll had also exhibited several years earlier) and her future career as a recorder of rural scenes was set. Throughout the 1890s and early 1900s Allingham toured Surrey, illustrating works such as *Happy England* (1903) and *The Cottage Homes of England* (1909), books which would have appealed to Jekyll, who had herself published *Old West Surrey* in 1904 (later to be republished as *Old English*

Thomas Hunn was one of many artists who chose to record the gardens at Munstead Wood. *The Pansy Garden* was a little-known area at Munstead and Hunn's view of the garden Is unique.

Household Life, 1925). Allingham's visit to Munstead Wood resulted in nine watercolours, including several of the famous south border and others of the single-species and seasonal borders, including the Michaelmas daisy border. The paintings are now scattered in different collections, including one in the Garden Museum, one in the Godalming Museum (which holds a special Jekyll collection), and one in the collection of the Royal Watercolour Society.

Another artist visitor to Munstead Wood was Thomas Hunn (1857–1928), who concentrated his watercolours on some of the lesser-known areas and working parts of the garden, including his depiction of *The Pansy Garden (Munstead Wood)*. Hunn also recorded the gardens at Great Tangley Manor, a favourite haunt of Jekyll, who greatly admired the water, bog and rock gardens, as well as the flower gardens all set around the moated timber-built manor. Jekyll described the water garden at Great Tangley as 'a paradise for flower lovers' and they appear so in Hunn's paintings.

In 1904 Jekyll collaborated with the artist George Samuel Elgood on the publication *Some English Gardens*. Elgood (1851–1943) was by then a highly regarded garden artist specialising, as Jekyll noted in the opening sentence of the book, in 'The English gardens which … have come down to us through the influence of the Italian Renaissance' although 'modified by gradual and insensible evolution into what has become an English style'. Brought up in the industrial city of Leicester, Elgood had studied at the South Kensington

Great Tangley Manor, seen here in the painting by Thomas Hunn, was one of Gertrude Jekyll's favourite places.

George Samuel Elgood worked with Gertrude Jekyll on the book *Some English Gardens*. This slightly different version of Elgood's *Gardens of the Dean of Rochester* appeared in another popular work of the time.

Schools of Art, returning to his home town before then travelling in Europe. From the 1890s onwards he was perhaps the most successful artist of the 'old-world' gardens of stone-edged pools, topiary, yew hedges and bowling greens, sometimes even peopling them with eighteenth-century characters. Elgood settled in Tenterden, Kent, in the early 1900s and this closer geographical connection appears to have been influential in his collaboration with Jekyll, as well as their mutual friendship with Dean Hole, the rosarian, although Elgood had already painted Dean Hole's garden at Rochester in the 1890s.

Many of the paintings in the book were commissioned especially, and Elgood chose to paint Gertrude Jekyll's Michaelmas daisy border for inclusion (although the border had already been recorded by Helen Allingham). While Elgood was at Munstead in 1900 he coincidentally showed around writers from *Country Life* and *The Studio,* one of whom recorded the visit: 'Up and down this sheltered alley did the writer walk with Mr Elgood, that most excellent of garden painters, discussing the kindness of Miss Jekyll, the beauty of her house and of her garden and the wood in which it stands, and behold they were very good.' Elgood was later to follow Jekyll's design ideals when creating his own garden at Knockwood, Tenterden, with his wife, Mary. Jekyll was paid £100 for the text of *Some English Gardens*, a rare insight into her financial dealings at this period of her life, when much of her income was from book writing and nursery sales direct to clients. Income from these sales could be substantial; the plants for Barrington Court, Somerset, were to be billed at £400, for example (approximately the equivalent of £23,000 in 2010) and invoices to other clients demonstrate the very substantial numbers of plants involved.

This invoice from the Munstead Wood nursery to Mrs Redhead at Great House Hambledon, Surrey, reveals planting of *Lychnis*, *Echinops* and giant *Eryngium* as well as *Laurustinus*, roses, etc.

The plant list for the Great House reveals a concentration on plants with grey foliage. The handwriting here is markedly worse than the accompanying invoice for the same site.

Many of the plants which Jekyll listed as available from the Munstead nursery were traditional, cottage-style garden plants, but others were of a more specialist nature and included those brought from abroad by herself or other plant hunters. There was already a 'reserve garden' for the reception of new plants and seedlings at Munstead House in 1882, including areas where plants could be reared and divided for restocking the rest of the garden or passing on to friends; William Robinson received bags of trilliums, daffodils and grape hyacinth there in 1883, sent from California and awaiting their onward journey to his own gardens, not yet established.

The nursery at Munstead Wood was first mentioned by the writer Theresa Earle in 1897, when she said that 'Miss Jekyll of Munstead Wood … now sells her surplus plants, all more or less suited to light soils'. It was to remain part of her life (and income) until her death in 1932, and subsequently was run by her nephew, Francis Jekyll, for a further nine years. Only one copy of the nursery catalogue is known to survive, a small fifteen-page booklet with shrubbery, border and alpine plants, as well as the Munstead flower basket and Munstead Wood pot-pourri. It contains only 324 plant varieties, a limited range in comparison with those we might now expect from a nursery, but one which included almost all of her signature design plants – and it was her own design commissions that provided much of the sales.

At Munstead Wood itself there was a 'top nursery' and a 'lower nursery', as well as plants being available from within the species gardens. An account book suggests that Jekyll provided plants for many of the 398 projects recorded, and a complex system of notation on plans and accounts indicates whether plants were to come from her nurseries or from specialists such as Jackman or Gauntlett (who specialised in Japanese-style gardens). It was through these plant sales that much of her money was actually made and the scale of the sales is astounding. In May 1911, for example, she supplied six hundred plants from her nursery to the new gardens she designed at Durbins, Guildford, Surrey, for the artist Roger Fry. The garden was described as being predominantly pinks, blues and greys with Canterbury bells, catmint (*Nepeta*) and 'Monthly' (China) roses. The plants

that came from the nursery included fifty-four *Nepeta* and forty-two *Santolina* as well as eighteen *Yucca filamentosa*. For the Sitwells' family home at Renishaw Hall, Derbyshire, she supplied over two thousand plants, including two hundred and fifty of her 'special strain' of snapdragons in colours from pale pink to lemon white. In the Renishaw long alley, beds were filled with marigolds, maize, cannas and dahlias, giving bright oranges and reds, and the garden was described by Osbert Sitwell as 'in gala this year'. In the following year thousands of plants went to Hydon Ridge, Hambledon, Surrey, and Fairhill, Berkhamsted, Hertfordshire – the latter including 388 *Iris* and 278 *Stachys*.

Designed in her Munstead years, this flower basket designed and made by Jekyll displays her Arts and Crafts versatility.

Work within the nursery (and the gardens) was carried out by Jekyll herself, as well as her team of gardeners. In *Wood and Garden* she describes dividing primroses:

> All day for two days I sit on a low stool dividing the plants. A boy feeds me with armfuls of newly dug-up plants, two men are digging-in the cooling cow-dung at the farther end, and another man carries away the divided plants tray-by-tray and carefully replants them.

Jekyll frequently used architectural plants and foliage plants within her flower borders. *Yucca gloriosa* was one of her favourites, appearing in her plant designs and at Munstead Wood itself.

Amongst all the plants in the nursery were a considerable number which she herself had selected and bred to obtain improved varieties. Some, such as the *Lupinus polyphyllus* 'Munstead' variety, or her own Munstead poppies, both registered at Kew, have subsequently been lost to cultivation, but about twenty-five others still survive. These range from the relatively well known, such as *Nigella damascena* 'Miss Jekyll Blue' and 'Miss Jekyll White' or *Lavandula spica* 'Munstead', to the less familiar *Paeonia decora* 'Gertrude Jekyll'. Many bear the name of Munstead House or Munstead Wood (*Aquilegia vulgaris* 'Munstead White', or *Pulmonaria*

NIGELLA MISS JEKYLL

Nigella damascena 'Miss Jekyll' is one of many plant varieties named after her. Some were bred or improved by her at Munstead Wood; others were named in honour of her work.

angustifolia azurea 'Munstead Blue'), while others, such as *Nigella damascena* 'Miss Jekyll Blue' are clearly named after her. Not all were raised by Jekyll, some being named after her by others, for example the *Narcissus* 'Gertrude Jekyll' raised by the Reverend Nelson of Aldborough, Norfolk, and illustrated in *The Garden* in 1883. Through her nursery, and her new varieties of plants, Gertrude Jekyll influenced even more gardens than those she actually designed. As someone who grew plants for sale, Jekyll could, by 1897, no longer claim to be an 'amateur' within the strict definitions of the term imposed by the Royal Horticultural Society or societies linked to it. She was, however, still able to win prestigious awards for the various varieties that she grew. In 1899 she received an RHS Award of Merit for *Viola* 'Jackanapes'; in 1901 a similar award went to Munstead bunch primrose, 'The Sultan'; another bunch of Munstead primroses won the Banksian Medal in 1901.

After the construction of Munstead Wood, Gertrude Jekyll's commitments there, combined with her much deteriorated eyesight, meant that she rarely travelled to commissions beyond the south of England. However, that did not lessen the demand for her services. In addition to work in Ireland and Scotland, there were requests from Europe and from as far afield as Algiers and North America. In France she designed gardens at Le Bois des Moutiers, Normandy, for the family of Guillaume Mallet, who desired a garden in the English style to complement the Lutyens-designed house. A very different commission, for the Parc des Sports Versailles, came almost thirty years later, where the

Lavandula angustifolia 'Munstead', raised by Gertrude Jekyll and available in her nursery catalogue as *Lavandula spica* 'Munstead'.

client James Hyde apologised for the small area allowed for flowers among his running track and tennis courts! In Algiers she planted the fountain gardens of Djenan-el-Mufti, which were then featured in her book *Garden Ornament* (1918), while in the United States she produced planting plans for gardens at Elmhurst, Ohio, in 1914, Cotswold Cottage, Connecticut, in 1925 and Old Glebe House, Woodbury, Connecticut, in 1926. Her influence abroad was such that visitors from other countries beat a path to the garden gates of Munstead, requesting interviews and prompting her to declare that 'If only I knew who were the genuine applicants, I would still make exceptions. You can have no idea how I have suffered from Americans, Germans and journalists.'

Elephant's ears (*Bergenia cordifolia*) was another of Jekyll's favourites, providing year-round foliage when used as edging.

The First World War had an enormous impact on the art, culture and creativity that had typified the first decade of the new century. The Edwardian heyday, hanging on after the death of Edward VII, crashed around Jekyll and Lutyens as it did so many others. Commissions were cancelled or changed as economic circumstances altered and, with the loss of a generation, so many properties lacked heirs. Writing to an American friend in 1919, Jekyll declared that 'The War has brought me an altered life. The cost of labour is ruinous', and Vita Sackville-West, visiting Munstead in 1917, noted that the gardens were not at their best. A more unexpected aspect of architecture and gardening in the aftermath of the war years was in the commemoration of the fallen. Shortly after the outbreak of the First World War, Sir Fabian Ware, appalled by the massive losses of life and the unrecorded graves, had formed what was to become the Imperial War Graves Commission (later renamed the Commonwealth War Graves Commission). The Commission created walled cemeteries for the fallen, each man commemorated by an identical headstone. Involving architect (and author of *The Formal Garden in England*) Sir Reginald Blomfield, and literary advisor Rudyard Kipling, the Commission also sought advice from Edwin Lutyens and Gertrude Jekyll. Lutyens designed what would come to be known as the 'Stone of Remembrance' (placed in every cemetery with over one thousand burials), while Jekyll recommended combinations of planting reflecting, as far as possible, the gardens of the original country of the fallen. Following the success of the initial cemetery at Forceville, France, this became the pattern for the majority of the twenty-three thousand sites which exist today across one hundred and fifty countries. Sir Frederick Kenyon, co-ordinating the designs, believed that 'There is no reason why cemeteries should be places of gloom', and Jekyll's planting uplifted and soothed the thousands who visited those earlier cemeteries during the 1920s and 1930s.

AUTUMN OF A
GARDENING LIFE

IN THE MID 1920s, despite being then in her eighties, Gertrude Jekyll was designing as many as eight to ten gardens a year as well as continuing to advise on some of her earlier garden designs. In 1923 she embarked, after a hiatus of fifteen years, on a further commission with Lutyens, who had just completed the prestigious and extensive New Delhi project. The joint commission at Gledstone Hall, Yorkshire, was to be a *tour de force*, combining Palladian-style architecture and formal structure with planting in an impressionistic style. Jekyll was not able to visit the site owing to increasing blindness but, as was by now her usual practice, requested samples of the soil and details of the type of stone and colours before producing her planting plans. A long canal, loggia, terraces, and pergola (never built) recall many of their earlier projects together, as did the combination plantings of *Stachys lanata*, monardas and lavenders. Stronger colours marked some of the more architectural areas of the garden, as they had done at Hestercombe, with red-hot pokers combining with the architectural foliage of *Acanthus mollis* and *Bergenia cordifolia*. Not all of the planting was as successful in Yorkshire as it had been in Somerset. Some of the plants that were sent up from the Munstead nursery had to be replaced, and designs tweaked during the course of the project to account for the difference in climate. Thousands of plants were shipped by rail from Surrey to Yorkshire, all packed with care at Munstead by Jekyll herself or overseen by her. In 1928 she invoiced the client, Sir Amos Nelson, £93 for plants as well as 105 guineas for her design fee (the latter being a professional fee, it was of course calculated in guineas). Although these were relatively substantial sums for the period, Jekyll was increasingly concerned about her financial situation, perhaps influenced by the near bankruptcy of her close friend Ellen Willmott, once fabulously wealthy but by this time forced to sell most of her assets to survive.

The 1920s also brought royal recognition in the form of a commission to design the garden for Queen Mary's Dolls' House. Again Lutyens had been requested to design the house, including the minute garden, complete with garden pots an inch high. Jekyll filled in the 'planting', specifying harmony

Opposite:
Miss Jekyll in the spring garden at Munstead Wood in the final years of her life.

41

Despite her increasing age, the 1920s were a busy decade for Jekyll, who kept up a steady stream of cuttings, etc., as demonstrated by her garden notebook for the period.

White Japanese anemones catch the eye in this vision of the ideal Edwardian pergola using local stone and hardy plants at Hestercombe, Somerset.

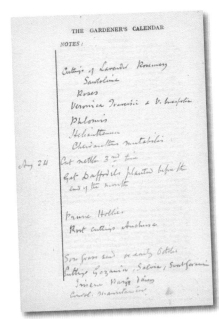

with the pots and noting dissatisfaction with their overall shape in a letter of 17 March 1923.

Although the majority of her gardening books had been written in the earlier part of her gardening career, the mid-1920s saw a return to interest in the household arts, design and crafts. In 1924 Jekyll revised and enlarged her 1904 work *Old West Surrey*, finally republishing it as *Old English Household Life* in 1925. She also wrote articles for the periodical *English Life* (to which Lutyens also contributed)

and the *Empire Review*, as well as the *Gardener's Chronicle*. In 1928 she published an article on 'The Changes of Fashion in Gardening' in the periodical *The Nineteenth Century* – who better to write it than a *grande dame* who had seen so much of that century! *Garden Ornament*, published in 1918, had also brought Jekyll to the attention of a slightly later generation, and one for whom the inter-war style of the more formal garden appealed, where statues and sundials proliferated even in the smaller suburban gardens of the rising middle classes. The American interest in Jekyll's style also continued unabated, and in 1926 she sent designs for 600 feet of flower border for the Glebe House, Connecticut (now recreated).

Miniature tulips made for Queen Mary's Dolls' House. The house itself was designed by Lutyens.

Jekyll-influenced planting can be seen in long borders in many gardens; here at Waterperry, Oxfordshire, mauves and yellows contrast and complement.

The last collaboration with Lutyens came in 1928, when Edward Hudson purchased an old moated manor house at Plumpton, Sussex, and brought together again the team that had provided him with the splendours of the

Deanery Gardens and the weekend retreat at Lindisfarne. Plumpton was a very different style and, again working with images and plans sent to her, Jekyll was able to dispatch planting schemes promptly for both the more formal borders and the wild areas of the gardens. The wild areas in particular demonstrate how mentally active she still was, despite now being eighty-five, switching from formal to informal instinctively. To complement the simple and natural look that Hudson desired, she suggested *Clematis vitalba*, tall white foxgloves, and '*Iris P bastardi*', alongside mixed ferns, primulas, and 'a few thousand columbines' – to be provided of course from the stocks at Munstead. Christopher Hussey, writing in 1933, praised this naturalistic planting, although failed to mention its designer!

Another of Jekyll's final gardens was at Durford Edge, Hampshire, for a house originally created by Inigo Triggs in 1911. Details of planting for a rose garden, shrub borders and walls survive, along with a note of gratitude from the owner, the professor of mathematics John Percy Gabbat, dated 1926. The work was considerably more extensive than the flower border planting schemes which she most often produced for clients by this period of her life, and Jekyll had suggested that some of the plants might come from her local Godalming nurseries. The Gabbats were fortunate to capture one of the final blooms of her creativity so close to the end of Jekyll's own life. Although the

Gertrude Jekyll is instantly recognisable by her hat, glasses and apron in this modern cartoon by Greg Becker.

pace and scale of work inevitably slowed, records show that Jekyll continued to provide smaller-scale planting plans for clients into her final years. Woodhouse Copse, Surrey, received plans in 1926–8 for the flower borders, which Jekyll declared were 'rather too short' (at 68 feet) for good effect. In the same year (1928) she designed for Blagdon Hall, Northumberland, where the client, Viscount Ridley, was married to Ursula, daughter of Edwin Lutyens. In 1928 she was awarded a Gold Veitch memorial medal by the Royal Horticultural Society for her services to horticulture and gardening. Marylands, Hurtwood, Surrey, occupied her in 1929, and her papers record preliminary work on a further site in the year of her death, 1932, although it was also noted by a visitor to Munstead in that year that the shrubs and borders were looking rather overgrown.

In her final years Jekyll often mentioned her age and her increasing ill health in letters to her friends and prospective visitors. Tiredness and 'heart strain' were the main problem: she wrote to Viscountess Wolseley in May 1925 that visitors would have to come after 3.30 p.m., as 'I am obliged to have a complete rest in the earlier afternoon'. In the summer of 1932 she made use of an invalid chair (given to her by Lutyens) in order to progress around the gardens – although when her lifelong friend Mr Pearsall Smith visited that summer she commented to him that '... there's a big patch of blue *Meconopsis* behind the tool shed you might like to see. I'm sorry I can't come and show it to you.' A letter in the August of that year explains to the recipient that 'my doctor keeps me very close on account of a worn-out heart, so that many things that I ought to do have to be set aside'. Visiting in 1931, however, the garden writer, designer and landscape architect Russell Page found 'A dumpy figure in a heavy gardener's apron, her vitality shining from a face half concealed behind two pairs of spectacles and a battered and yellowed straw hat'.

At the end of September 1932 Jekyll's beloved brother Herbert died suddenly, and it was not long after her own eighty-ninth birthday in the November that she also fell ill. Two weeks later, on 8 December 1932, Gertrude Jekyll finally laid down her writing pen and trowel and died peacefully at Munstead. She was buried at St John the Baptist church, Busbridge, on 12 December 1932 after a service attended by both of her lifelong gardening friends, William Robinson and Ellen

'The Michaelmas daisies are so important in September and October that it is well worth while to give them a separate place, in addition to their use with other flowers in the mixed border.' *Colour Planning of the Garden,* introduction by Gertrude Jekyll. Shown here at the Salutation Garden, Kent.

Jekyll's memorial was designed by Lutyens and incorporated tombstones for Miss Jekyll herself, her brother Herbert and his wife. A planting area now contains some of her hallmark plants.

Willmott — themselves both infirm (Robinson was in his nineties and confined to a chair, Willmott in her mid-seventies and recovering from pneumonia). Rather fittingly, the church contained a decorative altar frontal and stained glass by William Morris and Edward Burne-Jones.

The Times obituary for Gertrude Jekyll, published on 10 December 1932, highlighted not only her horticultural and artistic skills, but also her great patience with the horticulturally inexperienced who flocked to her doors, telling of visitors who requested 'some of those lovely flowers I saw in your garden last time I came; I think you called them Peacocks', who were duly and patiently rewarded, after some hard thinking, with *Narcissus pallidus praecox*! Another client, when questioned on the aspect of her border, had claimed that 'Most of the day it faces south-east, but due north all of the morning', surely drawing a quiet chuckle from the recipient of the note. In summing up her contribution *The Times* recorded that:

> She was a great gardener, second only, if indeed she was second, to her friend William Robinson of Gravetye. To these two, more than to any others, are due not only the complete transformation of English horticultural method and design, but also that wide diffusion of knowledge and taste which has made us almost a nation of gardeners.

Thirty years later, in 1962, William Robinson had been largely cast aside and Russell Page wrote: 'I can think of few gardens made in the last fifty years which do not bear the mark of [Gertrude Jekyll's] teaching.' In 1933, as a last service to his lifelong friend and partner, Edwin Lutyens designed a memorial for the grave with a simple inscription encapsulating her life and work:

> *Gertrude Jekyll*
> *November 1843*
> *December 1932*
> *'Artist*
> *Gardener*
> *Craftswoman'*

A GARDENING LEGACY

And as the quick years pass and the body grows old around the still young
heart, and the day of death grows ever nearer; with each new springtide the
sweet flowers come forth and bloom afresh...

'Epilogue' from *A Gardener's Testament*, Country Life, 1937.

B Y THE OUTBREAK of the Second World War in 1939, almost all the great
gardeners, designers, architects and artists who had once moved in Jekyll's
circle, or she in theirs, were gone, some after her, some predeceasing her: John
Ruskin (d. 1900); the Reverend Wolley Dod, described by Gertrude Jekyll as
'scholar, botanist and gentleman' (d. 1904); Hercules Brabazon (d. 1906);
Harry Mangles (d. 1908); Canon Ellacombe (d. 1916); Theresa Earle (d. 1925);
Ellen Willmott (d. 1935); William Robinson (d. 1935); Viscountess Wolseley
(1936); and finally Edward Hudson (d. 1936), marking the end of the first
Country Life era. Only the young Lutyens, caught between generations, lived
beyond that 'golden afternoon', dying in 1944. The house and gardens at
Munstead Wood were left to Aggie, Herbert's widow, who herself died in 1937.
Gertrude Jekyll's nephew Francis moved into Munstead Wood and kept up the
gardens and nursery for the following years, but economic conditions did not
favour a large family home and small business, and the estate
was broken up and sold in 1948.

Rosa 'Gertrude
Jekyll', a David
Austin rose
created in 1978
and named in her
honour. The rose
has a glorious
scent and will
flourish as a
rambler or in
the borders.

Although her generation had passed on, Gertrude Jekyll
left behind a legacy of her gardens, her abundant writings,
and her lasting influence on later designers and garden
owners. This influence can be clearly seen in the work of
the following generation such as Vita Sackville-West, Norah
Lindsay, Nancy Lancaster and Margery Fish, while the rose
gardens and herbaceous borders of Graham Stuart Thomas
spread the Jekyll influence through many National Trust
properties. Graham Stuart Thomas, Gardens Adviser to the
National Trust for thirty years, was himself an artist as well

Two aspects of
Gertrude Jekyll's
life are captured
side by side in the
Garden Museum:
her writing desk
and her garden
desk.

as a garden designer, writer, and recipient of both the RHS Victoria Medal of Honour and the Veitch Memorial Medal – echoing thereby many of the achievements of Gertrude Jekyll.

In addition to designers influenced, wittingly or not, by her ideas of colour and planting, some of our most famous and loved gardens bear witness to her ideas. The White Garden at Sissinghurst, for example, was formed by Vita Sackville-West years after visiting Munstead Wood with her mother and Lutyens in 1917, when she met Jekyll and toured the 'grey garden'. At the time of the visit Vita recorded, 'Miss Jekyll rather fat and rather grumbly; garden not at its best, but can see it must be lovely'. Much later, when Vita's own gardening career was established, she described Jekyll in rather more complimentary terms as 'That grand gardener to whom we owe so much'. Another gardener who visited Munstead in its heyday, and was instrumental in promoting Jekyll's ideas to later generations, was the American garden writer Mrs Francis King. Mrs King's influence as the founder of the Garden Club of America was undoubtedly partly responsible for Jekyll being awarded the George Robert White Medal of Honor by the Massachusetts Horticultural Society in 1929 (Mrs King had herself been a recipient of the same award). From the United States Marian Coffin and Beatrix Farrand (then Beatrix Jones) also visited Munstead, and were to spread its influence across the Atlantic and to future generations. It was thanks to Beatrix Farrand that Jekyll's private papers, nursery lists and designs were saved for future researchers. In 1940 Francis Jekyll had offered the papers to the RHS for auction in a sale on behalf of the Red Cross, but the collection was, for unknown reasons, withdrawn at the last moment. In 1948, when the rest of the house and estate were sold, the papers, including 'the entire output of Gertrude Jekyll's long and distinguished career, together with her own manuscript plans, many letters from and to her clients', were purchased by Beatrix Farrand and eventually transferred by her to the University of California at Berkeley, where they remain as an invaluable resource – in particular for those seeking to restore a Jekyll garden.

The impact of the Second World War, and changing fashions in the 1960s and 1970s, meant that many of the gardens Jekyll designed were either neglected or in some instances destroyed in the mid- to late twentieth century. Some, however, survived, most often where associated with a Lutyens house, and over the last few decades restorations have been undertaken including those at Hestercombe (Somerset), Lindisfarne Castle (Northumberland), Townhill Gardens (Hampshire), and the stunning gardens at the Manor House, Upton Grey (Hampshire). In addition, smaller-scale restorations and recreations have been achieved: of the herb garden at Knebworth House (Hertfordshire); Hatchlands Park (Surrey); and Barrington Court (Somerset). Gardens such as Vann, Surrey, and Munstead Wood itself have developed from the original Jekyll schemes, but retain a wonderful Jekyllian atmosphere, perhaps even improved by

A classic Jekyll-style border at the Salutation Gardens, Kent.

their maturity. As these restorations have progressed they have furthered our understanding of her planting and design skills, while completed gardens showcase yet again her artistic talent and influence, encouraging a new generation to follow her. But it is perhaps in her writings that her legacy has been most marked. Although many of her articles for periodicals such as *The Garden* are now rarely read except by historians and academics, her books are still widely available and their wisdom and humour make them enduringly popular and rarely out of print.

In 1993 an exhibition on Gertrude Jekyll's life at the then Museum of Garden History, London, brought together archive material of the many different aspects of her life, from her sketches of her beloved cats and photographs of children and flowers, to the almost illegible plant lists and design plans. The discovery in the 1980s of forty-one booklets containing endless lists of plants, again in her challenging handwriting, extended our knowledge of her garden commissions and planting. These are retained in the Godalming Museum, Surrey, which also contains a special Jekyll exhibition, so not all is lost to the United States. Jekyll originally also designed a garden for the police station at Godalming, although sadly this is no longer in existence. In 2004 'The Hut', that temporary workplace designed by Lutyens, changed hands for £850,000, and other parts of the estate have become dissociated from the main gardens. In 2010 Jekyll's

A modern view of the garden court at Munstead Wood.

own designs for a series of flower vases, known as the Munstead Wood vases, were recreated, and achieved rapid popularity, a testament to her design skills. The Munstead flower basket for cut flowers, another of her designs, may also be revived.

Gertrude Jekyll's enduring impact and appeal have been based not only on her garden design, her artistic approach, and her writings, but also on an appreciation of her character as expressed through her writings. Unlike Robinson, who could be irascible and impatient, Jekyll's numerous books, articles and letters demonstrate great humour and an abiding love of friends, gardens and even the visiting strangers who invaded her solitude. Jekyll's fascination with the traditional architecture, gardens, plants and lifestyle of the English, and particularly the Surrey countryside, imbued her with an almost timeless quality. Forever 'Aunt Bumps'. Despite living through the reigns of Victoria, Edward VII and George V, she 'never grew old at heart or wearied in mind, was never discouraged by defeat or failure' and sought always for practical knowledge allied to beauty, transfiguring the gardens of England.

This combination of stone steps and *Erigeron karvinskianus* sums up the timeless effects produced by Lutyens and Jekyll, for whom *Erigeron* was a favourite plant.

This wonderful image entitled *Gertrude's Tea Party*, by the artist and allotment holder Greg Becker, demonstrates the continuing influence of Gertrude Jekyll in the modern day, and captures her love of innocent and childish pleasures.

A SELECTION OF GARDENS DESIGNED BY GERTRUDE JEKYLL IN PARTNERSHIP WITH EDWIN LUTYENS

Munstead Wood, 1883–1902
The Deanery Gardens, 1899–1901
Hestercombe, 1904–8
Barton St Mary, 1906
Tylney Hall, 1906
King Edward VII Sanatorium, 1907
The Manor House, Upton Grey, 1908
Rignall's Wood, 1909
Highmount, 1909–11
Lindisfarne Castle, 1911
Sandbourne, 1912
Frant Court, 1914
Felbridge Place, 1916
Durford Edge, 1923
Versailles (Parc des Sports), 1924
Gledstone Hall, 1923–5
The Court at St Fagans, 1925
The Old Lighthouse, 1925
Ickwell, The Old House, 1926–7
Blagdon Hall, 1928

No one knows for certain exactly how many gardens she actually designed or advised upon. There are records for about two hundred and fifty projects in her archives at the University of California, Berkeley, but Francis Jekyll lists three hundred and forty commissions.

Judith Tankard, *Country Life*.

PLACES TO VISIT

Barrington Court, near Ilminster, Somerset TA19 0NQ. National Trust.
Telephone: 01460 242614. Website:
www.nationaltrust.org.uk/main/w-barringtoncourt
(1920s home of Sir Arthur Lyle: Jekyll-influenced gardens.)

Castle Drogo, Drewsteignton, near Exeter, Devon EX6 6PB
Telephone: 01647 433306. Website: www.nationaltrust.org.uk

Durmast House, Burley, Hampshire BH24 4AT. Privately owned. Open
under the National Gardens Scheme. Website: www.ngs.org.uk
(Recently renovated following Jekyll's original plans.)

The Garden Museum, Lambeth Palace Road, London SE1 7LB
Telephone: 020 7401 8865. Website: www.gardenmuseum.org.uk

Glebe House Museum and Gertrude Jekyll Garden, Woodbury, Connecticut,
06798 USA. Telephone: 00 1 212 462 7820. Website:
www.theglebehouse.org
(Designed by Jekyll in 1926; one of her few American designs.)

Godalming Museum, 109a Godalming High Street, Godalming, Surrey GU7
1AQ. Telephone: 01483 426510. Website: www.waverley.gov.uk/
godalmingmuseum
(Includes an archive of Jekyll's garden drawings, plant list notebooks
and correspondence, as well as personal memorabilia and images.)

Guildford Museum, Castle Arch, Guildford, Surrey GU1 3SX.
Telephone: 01483 444751. Website: www.guildford.gov.uk/museum
(Permanent display on Gertrude Jekyll.)

Hatchlands Park, East Clandon, Guildford, Surrey GU4 7RT. National Trust.
Telephone: 01483 222482. Website:
www.nationaltrust.org.uk/main/w-hatchlandspark
(Small parterre garden by Gertrude Jekyll.)

Hestercombe Gardens, Cheddon Fitzpaine, Taunton, Somerset TA2 8LG.
Telephone: 01823 413923. Website: www.hestercombe.com
(Thought to be one of the best collaborations between Jekyll and
Lutyens, fully restored.)

Knebworth House, Knebworth, Hertfordshire SG3 6PY.
Telephone: 01438 812661. Website: www.knebworthhouse.com
(Small herb garden by Gertrude Jekyll.)

Le Bois des Moutiers, Route de l'Eglise, 76119 Varengeville sur Mer, France.
Telephone: 02 35 85 10 02. Website: www.boisdesmoutiers.com
(Jekyll gardens and Lutyens house in Normandy.)

Lindisfarne Castle, Holy Island, Berwick-upon-Tweed, Northumberland
TD15 2SH. National Trust. Telephone: 01289 389244.
Website: www.nationaltrust.org.uk/ lindisfarne

The Manor House, Upton Grey, Hampshire RG25 2RD.
Open by prior appointment only. Website:
www.gertrudejekyllgarden.co.uk
(House altered for Charles Holme, founder of Arts and Crafts magazine
The Studio. Gardens by Jekyll now fully and authentically restored.)

Owlpen Manor, near Uley, Gloucestershire. Privately owned, open to the
public. Telephone: 01453 860261. Website: www.owlpen.com
(Tudor house restored by the Arts and Crafts architect Norman Jewson
in 1925. The house and gardens were much praised by Jekyll in *Gardens
for Small Country Houses*.)

Salutation Gardens, Sandwich, Kent. Website: www.the-secretgardens.co.uk
(Gardens in the style of Gertrude Jekyll around a Lutyens house.)

Townhill Park House and Gardens, now owned by the Gregg School,
Southampton. Open to the public on selected days each year.
Website: www.st-winifreds-school.co.uk/greggs/gardens/townhill-
park.asp
(Recent restoration of Jekyll gardens.)

Surrey History Centre, 130 Goldsworth Road, Woking, Surrey GU21 6ND.
Telephone: 01483 518737. Website: www.surreycc.gov.uk/
surreyhistorycentre
(Includes letters, manuscripts, copies of photographic albums, plans etc.)

Vann, Hambledon, Godalming, Surrey GU8 4EF. Open by appointment
and under the National Gardens Scheme (NGS).
Telephone: 01428 683413. Website: www.vanngarden.co.uk
(Delightful Jekyll garden, grading from formal to wild and woodland.)

'Old English' style houses and gardens, such as here at Owlpen, Gloucestershire, were much admired by the Arts and Crafts Movement; Jekyll used topiary in her own garden at Munstead Wood.

FURTHER READING

Beyond the Borders: An Exhibition on the Work of Gertrude Jekyll, Artist, Gardener, Craftswoman. Surrey History Centre, 1999.

Bisgrove, Richard. *Gertrude Jekyll's Colour Schemes for the Flower Garden.* Frances Lincoln Ltd, 1988.

Bisgrove, Richard. *The Gardens of Gertrude Jekyll.* Frances Lincoln Ltd, 1992.

Brown, Jane. *Gardens of a Golden Afternoon: The Story of a Partnership: Edwin Lutyens and Gertrude Jekyll.* Allen Lane, 1982.

Eckstein, Eve. *George Samuel Elgood.* Alpine Fine Arts Collection Ltd, 1995.

Elgood, Samuel, and Jekyll, Gertrude. *Some English Gardens.* Country Life, 1904.

Festing, Sally. *Gertrude Jekyll.* Viking, 1992.

Gertrude Jekyll 1843–1932: A Celebration. Museum of Garden History, 1993.

Jekyll, Gertrude. *Wood and Garden.* Longmans Green & Co, 1899.

Jekyll, Gertrude. *Home and Garden.* Longmans Green & Co, 1900.

Jekyll, Gertrude. *Lilies for English Gardens.* Country Life, 1901.

Jekyll, Gertrude. *Children and Gardens.* Longmans Green & Co, 1908.

Jekyll, Gertrude. *The Beauties of a Cottage Garden.* Penguin Books, 2009.

Jekyll, Gertrude, and Weaver, Lawrence. *Gardens for Small Country Houses.* Country Life, 1912.

Lewis, Cherry. *The Making of a Garden* (anthology). The Antique Collectors' Club, 1984.

Massingham, Betty. *Miss Jekyll: Portrait of a Great Gardener.* David & Charles, 1973.

Massingham, Betty. *Gertrude Jekyll.* Shire Publications (Lifelines 37), 1975.

Ridley, Jane. *Edwin Lutyens: His Life, His Wife, His Work.* Pimlico, 2002.

Tankard, Judith. *Gertrude Jekyll and the Country House Garden.* Arum Press, 2011.

Tankard, Judith, and Wood, Martin. *Gertrude Jekyll at Munstead Wood.* Sutton Publishing, 1996.

Tooley, Michael, and Arnander, Primrose. *Gertrude Jekyll: Essays on the life of a Working Amateur.* Michaelmas Books, 1995.

Way, Twigs. *Virgins, Weeders and Queens: A History of Women in the Garden.* Sutton Publishing, 2006.

WEBSITES

www.gertrudejekyll.co.uk (The official website of the Jekyll estate.)

www.lutyenstrust.org.uk

www.ced.berkeley.edu/cedarchives/profiles/jekyll.htm (The digitised online collection of Jekyll presentation drawings, planting plans, plant lists, garden photographs and other material held at the University of California, Berkeley.)

INDEX

Page numbers in italics refer to illustrations

Allingham, Helen *cover, 2,* 33, 34
America (Jekyll gardens in) 39, 43
Ardilaun, Lady 22, 23
Arts and Crafts Movement 12, 14, 16, 27, 30, 54
Barrington Court *35,* 49, 53
Benson, Lionel *12,* 12
Berkeley Square 5,
Blagdon Hall 45
Blomfield, Reginald 24, 39
Bloomsbury Group 33
Blumenthal, Jacques 7, 8
Bodichon, Madame neé Leigh Smith 7, 8
Brabazon, Hercules 7, 13, 47
Bramley House 5, 6, 11
Burne-Jones, Edward 13, 46
Chinthurst Hill 16
Coffin, Marian 48
Cotswold Cottage, Connecticut, USA 39
Country Life 20, 29, 31, 47
Crooksbury, Surrey 16
Deanery Gardens, Sonning, Berks 19, 24, 27, 31, 44, 52
Djenan-al-Mufti, Algiers 39
Dod, Rev. Wolley 47
Drystone walls *25, 25,* 26
Durbins 37
Durford Edge 44
Durmast House, Burley 53
Earle, Marie Theresa 20, 21, 23, 27, 47
Edinburgh Review 19, 24
Edward VII Sanatorium *23,* 23
Elgood, George Samuel 19, 33, 34, *35,* 35
Ellacombe, Canon 47
Elmhurst, Ohio, USA 39
English Life 42
Fairhill, Berkhamsted 37
Farrand, Beatrix 48
Fish, Margery 48
Folly Farm, Sulhamstead 28
Formal gardens 24
Fry, Roger 33, 37

Gardener's Chronicle 43
Gauntlett nursery 36
Girton College, Cambridge 7
Glebe House, Connecticut, USA 43
Gledstone Hall, Yorkshire 41, 52
Glynde School for Lady Gardeners *22, 23,* 23
Godalming Branch, Women's Suffrage 21, *21*
Gravetye Manor *12,* 12, 46
Great House, Hambledon 36
Great Tangley Manor *34,* 34
Hampton Lodge 19
Hatchlands Park 49, 53
Hestercombe 9, *27, 28,* 30, 41, 48, 52, 53
Hole, Dean Samuel Reynolds 13, 22, 35
Hudson, Edward 29, 31, 43, 44, 47
Hunn, Thomas *32,* 33, 34
Hussey, Christopher 44
Hydon Ridge 37
Jackman nursery 36
Jekyll, Agnes 7, 47
Jekyll, Francis 36, 47, 48, 52
Jekyll, Gertrude
  Arts and crafts by 7, 8, *8,* 13, *37;* books by 19–20, 22, 23, 24, 33, 35, 37, 39, 42, 43; childhood 5–7; failing eyesight 9, 14, 38; financial affairs 35, 39, 41; illness 45; images of *Title Page, 4, 12, 18, 41, 44, 51;* legacy 47–51; nicknames 16, 17, 21; photography 13, 14; plants bred by/named after 37–8, *38;* signature planting 28, 29, *36,* 37, *38,* 39, 41, 43, *45,* 48, 49, 51; travel 6–8
Jekyll, Herbert 6, 7, 11, 13, 22, 45, 47
Jekyll, Joseph 6–8
Johns, Rev. C. A. 5, 6,
King, Mrs Francis 11, 48
Kingdon-Ward, Frank 22
Kipling, Rudyard 39
Knebworth House 49, 53
Lambay Castle 29

Lancaster, Nancy 48
Layard, Sir Henry Austen 7
Le Bois des Moutiers, Normandy *26,* 27, 38, 53
Leighton, Lord 8
Leslie, George 7, 8, 11
Lindisfarne Castle 29, 31, 44, 48, 52, 53
Louise, HRH, Princess 8, 16
Lutyens, Edwin 6, 11, 14, 16, 17, 23, 24, 27, 28, 29, 31, 38, 39, 41, 43, 45, 46, 47, 48, 50, 51, 52
Lutyens, Lady Emily (neé Lytton) 16, 21
Lytton, Constance 21
Mangles, Harry 14, *13,* 47
Marsh Court 27
Mendelssohn 7
Millmead House 6, 27
Morris, William 7, 11, 16, 46
Munstead House 11, 12, 13, 14, 15, 16, 22, 36, 37
Munstead Wood (see also 'Nursery') *2, 3,* 6, *10,* 13, *14,* 14, *17,* 17, 19, 20, 23, 24, 27, 29, 30, *32,* 33, 34, 36, 37, 38, *40,* 45, 47, 48, *50,* 52
Newton, Charles and Mary 7, 9
Nicholson, Sir William *Title Page, 2,*
Nursery, Munstead Wood 30, 35, *36,* 36, 37, 38, 41, 44
Old Glebe House, Woodbury, Connecticut, USA 39
Owlpen *54,* 54
Page, Russell 45, 46
Parc des Sports, Versailles, France 38, 52
Peto, Harold 16
Plumpton Place 31, 43
Queen Mary's Dolls House 41–2, *43*
Red House 16
Renishaw Hall 37
Robinson, William 11, 12, 13, 19, 21, *22,* 23, 36, 45–6, 47, 51
Rossetti, Dante Gabriel 13
Royal Horticultural Society (RHS) 13, 22, 38, 45, 48

Ruskin, John 7, 11, 13, 21, 47
Sackville-West, Vita 39, 47, 48
Salutation Garden *45, 49,* 54
Sissinghurst 48
Sitwell (family) 37
South Kensington Schools of Art 6, 15, 21
Standen 16
Stevenson, Robert Louis 7
Surrey (landscape) 5, 6, 11, 12, 14, 33, 51
The 'Hut' (Munstead Wood) 6–8, 16, 17, 50
The Garden 11, 12, 19, 38, 50
The Guardian 19, 20
The Manor House, Upton Grey *25, 30,* 30, *31,* 49, 52, 53
The Times 46
Thomas, Graham Stuart 48
Thursley 16
Tipping, H. Avray 31
Townhill Gardens 48, 49, 54
Triggs, Inigo 44
Vann 30, 49, 54
Victoria Medal of Honour (RHS) 22, 23, 48
von Arnim, Elizabeth 22–3
War Graves Commission (Imperial/ Commonwealth) 39
Wargrave 8, 11, 12
Warley Place 21
Waterperry *43*
Watts, G. F. 7
Weaver, Lawrence 20, 29
Webb, Philip 16
Westbury Court 29
White, Miss Henrietta 22
Wild gardens 24, 29, 30, 44
Willmott, Ellen 21, 22, *22,* 23, 41, 45–6, 47
Wolseley, Lady 19
Wolseley, Viscountess, Frances 45, 47
Woodhouse Copse 45
Woodland gardens 30